My Aunts at Twilight Poker

EAMONN WALL

Published in 2023 by
Salmon Poetry
Cliffs of Moher, County Clare, Ireland
Website: www.salmonpoetry.com
Email: info@salmonpoetry.com

ISBN 978-1-915022-37-0

Cover Image: *'Wetlands' by Jules McCue – julesmccue.com*
Cover Design & Typesetting: *Siobhán Hutson Jeanotte*

Printed in Ireland by Sprint Print

Salmon Poetry gratefully acknowledges the support of
The Arts Council / An Chomhairle Ealaíon

for

Juliette, Gavin, Cillian

Contents

Midday

cormorant
statuesque
on mud flats

grass bathed
bottle green

March sun

low Slaney
noontime

mother
you have left
this world

a week has flown

Swat

When I stretch to whip a French fry
from her plate
my granddaughter swats my hand
like this
SWAT SPIDER, she hisses.

My mother's whipping cream for strawberries.
I have escaped the yard to wallow
at her elbow.
I am held by a warning eye.
TEASPOON'S WORTH, mother says.

SWAT. I had moved my teaspoon into
mother's arc for a sly encore.
I am downed with a warning eye.
The wet tea towel mother's weapon of choice.

Granddaughter, you can bet your bottom dollar
I will stretch to free another French fry
from your plate. LIKE THIS.

WHISHT, my mother whispers.
Her index finger slyly shapes a cross below her nose.
She motions me forward toward the Pyrex bowl.

Yola Sprong

Ing Limerick, Cork, and var awye Donegal
Ich named bee sprong mot ich name sprong
Ich am kennen ing Co. Wexford, oor curneale
bunyane o 'Flemish, Yole Norstrum, Eerish
Grinnygoreek tale, gumshogue, ill consonants
zough vowels lidged ing laussod and sthoan
on boagher lethel leenen narrowe waudher wyse
Deight bee estuary gradjens and zea burd.

Ber in hoes gurt as kewe sthoan
venie speate to mee own wood faic
scud. Bee hash Wexford scuthcen
'Cham pealt douse feasogue dhen deemes
eedrowe ee wul and hull lick caabeen wish baan.
Chappy-time clepe, cham ee-drowe ta claam
wee spancel, croowe, skeagh, kewe
fidi zin lhygt is hash ee-drowe on venie
Nock waudher, men yuri yarra adh borde.
Na bonyee sprong is houle on laade
Baskeat ar buthther coolann vrem woork a zong.

Ee grinnygoreek fho cress a River Barrow
adh New Ross is myhene mize bee English
fan it ich am rumcht anseo: Dixons, Kavanaghs,
Doyles and Quirkes oor holly gee
tight ta yew and larch and elm. Cham
sprong, a strahanshair o' aam aul fan
mee name is cleped, a straayear beleaves
o' goouns houled in *Fahrenheit 451*;
mee zei grigs dap in ee deerling teoune
Oor *meitheal* creaped ing a yard
lick gazb vrem ee eepealthe kuddan skootch ing ire
lick aan yole holy zong, stholk men ta woork.
Vrem hye mee faic zoon zees zpeed:
Mot a zin gooude vriene clepe me neow ta life.

Sprong

In Limerick, Cork, and far off Donegal,
I go by pitchfork though it is as sprong
I am known in Co. Wexford, our corner
confluence of Flemish, Old Norse, Irish,
Cant, gibberish, many hard consonants
deep vowels lodged in wood and stone
on paths lining narrow waterways all
cleansed by estuary sediment and gull.

Borne in hands coarse as boot gravel
rank spittle to my own wood handle
rubbed. By harsh Wexford labourers
I am beaten banged cursed ten times
flung at wall and drain like old fish bone.
Dinner-time call, I am cast off to loiter
with motor, crow, skeagh, wellington
where sunlight is harshly cast on foul
bog water, men uproarious at table.
No bonny sprong is bounced on virgin
lap or oiled back from labour into art.

A visitor who crosses the River Barrow
at New Ross is dumbstruck by English
as it is spoken here: Dixons, Kavanaghs,
Doyles and Quirkes our holy offerings
Affixed to yew and larch and elm. I am
sprong, the strangest of them all: when
my name is called, the tourist thinks
of weapons raised in *Fahrenheit 451*;
my *ainm* heralds arrival in another space.
Our *meitheal* has gathered in the yard,
as dust from a beaten rug spreads to air
like an old psalm, on foot men to work.
From ditch my handle soon meets force:
But it is the sun that lures me back to life.

When Grandmother Came to Live with Us

When grandmother came to live with us,
mother told me once, she brought
but one small suitcase; all her adult life
having inhabited one guest room at the hotel
she had owned, granny liked to say
how confined space allowed for certain
freedoms to emerge, not to own or be
submerged in many accessories, shoes,
and clothes.

I recall still her elegance
of dress, how always her face and hands
sparkled with cleanliness.

Her husband,
a most contrary man, fitted his possessions
into twin containers: a worn brown valise
and shiny shaving bag to join our rowdy band:
visitors all traversing then a green and fertile land.

*

Lightly, grandmother walks downstairs
one hand like a girl's running
along the banister, the left
to her suitcase clutched, each step
emptying decades of attachments
like coppers dropped down
into heavy pails. She lands
in our kitchen of baking bread
and laundry horses, many children
laboring to be smart, and finds
a place between side window and fire.
She wore lace collars and favored dark attire.

Over time, we grew fast friends
seated hearth side, side plates balanced
on our knees, hands curved
through teacup handles. With some
dismay, I liked to watch as, first,
she spread butter across a slice of wheaten loaf;
then, reversed course to sweep
the Dairygold to one side. Why, Granny?
Though I did not dare to ask out loud.

I pass an hour this afternoon signing
many forms required to apply for Medicare,
drinking from a cup of Lyons' tea. Riding bikes
up and down the block, my neighbor's
children shout in frenzy and delight. As I
walk downstairs to get an envelope
and a book of stamps, I catch the light imprints
of your feet, Granny Annie, on talcum
powder shaken as evidence of a brighter life.

Grandmother Tugs the Drayman's Arm

A Horse misus'd upon the Road
Calls to Heaven for human blood.
William Blake

One morning, a Saturday as I suppose,
Crash, clink, clatter, roll and unholy oaths
Awoke Barrack St. At hilltop a blinkered
Dray, solid and silent as a hillock, stood
Stock still. Later, when her tears had dried
To memory, grandmother, in deep blue
Dress arrayed, declared that those bottles—
Beers and minerals contained in glass
And crate—had rolled from the drayman's
Cart the load incorrectly secured: culprit
Stout Steve Kelly, grey coat, red face,
Oiled hat. Cruel, grandmother said, her
Voice firmer now, to have whipped
That simple beast about its face and flank.
The unholy racket drew us children into
The road, grown-ups in pursuit. Later,
When the team from the beer distributor's
—Lett's or Donohoe's I don't recall—were
Done with sweeping up, we returned home.
Grandmother's tears ran hard the hollowed
Gaps of her tight cupped face. She shook.
I'd last heard her cry the day JFK had died.

*

Though the Slaney has deepened its rolling
Bed, grandmother retains her spot
On Barrack St., fixed between drayman's
Whip and blinkered beast. Perhaps, as I recall,
It has begun to rain, or the hill's been layered
In ice. Long from angina she had suffered.
I find her seated too in her kitchen spot—

Farthest from the door and closest to the fire—
That Saturday stout Steve Kelly beat about
A stone-still dray and hit and pulled and beat.
He whipped and flayed, and hit, and beat, hit
One more time, and more, everything carried,
Note for note, along the chill mid-morning air.
He cursed and shouted out such red-faced roars
Our Grandmother had absorbed only to disdain.
The noble beast standing solemnly stolid in the rain.

*

Grandmother tugs the drayman's arm. We
Were children then who waited for them
To separate, the scene bathed in slow, lucid
Light. Indoors, her sobbing ended, breath
Caught, face of color drained, I watched
Mother climb a stool to release a Power's
Gold Label from the highest cupboard shelf,
A drop to press medicinally into her mother's
Tea. Grandmother went about the house
Ghostily; she cherished tender calm the aged
Favour; she read her missal, recited her rosary,
Not once that day did she offer another word.

*

This morning, on a wall of our old house
On Barrack St., I take note of grandmother's
Image heralded cabinet high above sofa,
Mugs and telephone. She's seated on a white
Bench beside her brother Gerald in the garden
Of a chalet by the sea, these two for lifetimes
Holding warm because I can read it in their faces,
Happy, as I suspect, to seem children in eternity
Racing along the grooved potato drills for home.

Strangers Seated Together in Chili's at O'Hare

You are native to my old state. I seek
news of that warm territory. When you walked
the Dundee alleyways did you hail
my old brown home holding firm, my young
daughter in flight from service
as crossing guard at eponymous elementary
school? She is now a mother who fixes
a crockpot roast bathed in succulence, many
carrots and potatoes added just for my delight,
to her baby I shape faces, likely to seem the fool.

Traveler, do you note the waft and scent
of sage by our backyard fence in May? Do sandhill
cranes still traverse the silent land, geese
gather in thousands come November at De Soto Bend?

The Music Lovers

I trace the mourners' steps from the sexton's stile to Slaney Place. The café's wheaten loaves are formed into shape by wind blowing downriver from the Island Rd., and by a woman's gifted hands. Two stragglers settle in for lunch as rain begins to fall on Tom Doyle's grave on an idle plain above the Slaney, hemmed between hill and mountain.

Even to himself, Tom had to admit, he was a legend; town elders perched on high stools sang his graces with a football, defenders nutmegged, left on sullied arses with the dead. Many sought to emulate his liquid turns of phrase. Once, I bade farewell to him by intoning, "I'll see you around," to which Tom thundered, "You never know your luck in a small town." Full of irony and erudition, a diminutive oracle in an overcoat, he walked downhill to the river waving at all greeters. Lithe, pontifical, local Diego Maradona.

Our last conversation took place outside of Kavanagh's Bargain Shop on Irish St. We talked an hour of bands and songs as snow fell on his darkest of coats, across the street from where Mr. Horgan once stood in the doorway of the Irish St. Stores, as guardian and patron of my childhood. One of many of those in town who made a life of watching. Tom Doyle and I shared an interest in music.

A thought came to me as we talked: Tom reaching into his great coat to draw from his deep pockets *Unhalfbricking* and *Liege and Leaf*—vinyl, not CD—though this was just my fallacy. We parsed and parried all the songs in their proper order, Tom correcting any faulty attribution that I made. Was it true, I asked him, that the couple pictured on *Unhalfbricking*'s cover were Sandy Denny's parents?

We talked of what we loved—musicianship, songwriting, vocals—track by track from "Genesis Hall" to "Million Dollar Bash." We did not linger on Sandy Denny's "Who Knows Where the Time Goes," a work of beauty and passion so far beyond language that we feared degrading it with poorly chosen words. How could a woman of such youth achieve such wisdom, I wondered? I told Tom that I cry when I hear that song and so I never play it when others are present in the room. Tom looked skyward in agreement.

The light fading and wind rising on a winter's afternoon, we passed more quickly through *Liege and Leaf*: "Matty Groves" an epic we held over for another day. These songs that turn us inside out, that make the tenors of our soft selves visible to us, that reveal the luster of our ragged lives in simple rhyme and apt cliché, all held aloft by music.

In secret, pain is salved by the miracle of song, tears flow in majesty and triumph down our faces as our turntables make rotations in the dark. We embrace our weaknesses at thirty-three and one-third RPM and became men.

I am in St. Louis where I watch through spotted glass rain fall on fresh-cut grass. Water drops from hanging baskets that line the brick-lined pathway to the street. I imagine that the rain hits on the many long-playing records that Tom Doyle spun, then returned from turntable to sleeve in the rhythm of a life.

Across the street, a dogwood and a red bud tree have lately come into white and purple bloom. A cat is sleeping on my desk. The tea's gone cold. One will learn something of another's soul from his caress of vinyl. Instead of hurting the cardboard covers, the rain enhances tones and colors, Fairport Convention sounding better with the years. In my home, music never plays as background; it fills all rooms.

Tom Doyle's time of suffering has ended, his form is passing into shadow. The main body of mourners who had huddled close above Tom Doyle's grave now gather at John Doyle's rasher counter in the Duffry to begin the task of immortalizing his legend into lore.

Living at a great distance from the town, I join the mourners with a poem, walking among them from the cemetery, present while absent, my shoes bopping along Island Rd. to a café riverside for reminiscence with a friend. By the time our coffees have been served, Charon has journeyed half-way down the estuary, the bridges, grey herons, and cormorants passed from sight into memory. Everything is moving. Somewhere, carefully, a man removes a record from its sleeve.

Gyodo, Glendalough

i.m. Seamus Heaney

Tighter than a monastery cell is this airplane seat
I am planed and fitted to, pressed again toward Ireland.
If in cruciform my arms stretch left and right,
the steward's cart is halted, my neighbor's screen divided.
Up here, no blackbirds alight to settle in for nesting,
fields now visible across my sleeping companion's palms.

Cloudy, hazy, I walk the trails today of Glendalough
to purge the body, loose the mind of the tight confine
of the day before. Oaked and spruced, mist-sprinkled,
water warbled wood and sloping swept to lakeside,
all spirits now lurch to perch aloft, then drop to whip
to water waves of antic liberation, Seamus Heaney.
I am among fellow migrants safely landed home
to inbreathe fragrant prayers fathers ferry on the wind.

Morning, La Crosse

Riverside & La Crosse at breakfast hour:
yellow tents, runners on the promenade,
like guiding bones light craft shifting
indigently down the Mississippi. Though
distant, my father sings out from treetop:
eagles await, owls are falling into shadow.
All breath is sacred, on our buckled knees
our buildings stand proud breathing out
aspirations, bent out of shade toward sunlight,
lent down to the river. Sweet world, do you
love me still? Big Muddy where pilgrims
and prophets might gather to repent, wrench
of land fall bearing breath of indigenous
people who claiming nothing possessed all.
In La Crosse on a bench by the Mississippi
my father descended from his tree offers me
a wild woodbine. I catch in the red stone
on a far hill a glow of liquid, fiery, breathing
life. In Ireland long ago with ash and oak
we wrote our poems out on the waking land.

The Monks' Music

I was once a child who lived inside a monastery.
Many days—afternoon and evening walk
along cool lighted cloister—I passed
amongst gentle-souled Cistercians. I wound
my way under arches to the college chapel
to pray psalm and vesper in faith and resurrection.
I recall the core and wash of winter oak,
the wet flagstones, the chill marble
and gray brush of the holy water font
as I counted horae canonicae to winter break.

Snow has closed this Midwest city down.
Lit by sunlight, I cast slow hours wrapped
in my wide recliner. I turn pages
of Murakami's latest to free some weight
from the heavy hours, a sinker in the sand
below the angler's feathers and baited hooks.

Recently recorded, monks' chants sit on top
of Ireland's music charts, their songs and silence
ringing out across black and white Missouri,
revolving on my bookshelf player overhead:
Bach and Handel are blasted from recliner
to eternity. The snow on the grass caring not
one flake for St. Benedict or modernity.

The monks' music is warmer inside me now,
their sacred words have shed much harsh retort
just as heavy snows will erase inevitability's
hard and brutal lines. Wise, silent, sweeping tile
with habits as they strode, our monks outlined
other rhythms I required decades to encode.
Old and ancient Cistercians, I was an idle child
who fidgeted while you intoned. Outside, my street
is covered neat and deep with snow: many slow
hours to go till plows hit these roads. A choir
chants; monks reel lines to the rhythm of the waves.

Masculinity

One man's hand is placed
on top of another's hand
and fastened warmly;
this is a gesture that men
like my father made to press
a topic forward, to push it on
from commonage into
the private domain. I still feel
his solid hand rest on mine,
I sink into his trust, I turn
to him like an aspen branch
bent by wind, my leaves
lit and shimmering to absorb
the weight of his revelation.

*

Hand on hand was a mode
of speech among men I grew
up around; they were rough
and smooth, of farm and town.
I watched their heads incline,
bind together with their eyes.
I have crossed the ocean wide.

*

Once in a professional setting,
I placed my own hand on top
of a colleague's hand: my gesture
meant: I get it, Dude; I have
your back; the bossman, he's
a lousy jerk. The man recoiled.
The look he shot me would
have been no different had I
slapped him hard across his face
or kissed his lips. I stepped back
quick, into the corridor of shame.

Dear Charlotte, Emily, and Anne

We spent a rainy morning once
in Haworth, Yorkshire. We ran
uphill by leaning headstones,
then stood dripping rain onto
the floor of the historic parsonage.
Staff paid no heed many visitors
having traipsed sodden through
these rooms where the three
sisters dwelt in Angrias of finest
folded pages, tiny bodies, swift souls:
Rev. Brontë scribbled from desk
sermons by the thousands, his
poems among the pantheon today
at New York's Morgan Library,
one volume nestled beside another.
I imagine a trio formed for gray
viewing side-by-side on a train
platform, under an awning clock,
commuters crossing a walkway
who pause a moment to note
three models of odd assortment,
homespun clothes many decades
out-of-date. To Charlotte's
dress on view today late Victorians
attached for accent a darkest
widow's collar. We had walked
mesmerized among the rooms
at Haworth, tick-tack-tick of rain
pinging on pane and slate, the deep
moors from the sisters' pages
reduced to muted mystery strewn
beyond the perimeter steps, that
one June of floods, mayhem, all
England in celebration of the wise
sovereign's diamond jubilee.
These tiny forms, such genius!
Dear Charlotte, Emily, and Anne.

Alive in Autumn

A doe and fawn walk
along the border

between copse and grass

at the bottom of a hill.

Waves of geese drive southward.

Passing my spot, a child flies
along the borderline.

The copse waves. The deer
hold their ground, wary as thieves.

I live in an old
unwitnessed world.

Here, traipse of deer.
Here, herald of geese.

There! There!

My grandchild pausing to point.

There! There!

My Aunts at Twilight Poker

1.

The ground in front of Michael Collins' grave is covered in wreaths of flowers. One yellow coreopsis has been placed where the "Uncrowned King" of Ireland lies.

De Valera's grave is hard to find—I seek it out to favor my father who earlier this year left this world for eternity. Someone leads me a mazy walk along the avenues, my godmother the chief suspect: she was General O'Duffy and Garret FitzGerald to her core.

Other memorials and graves are easier to locate. I linger in Glasnevin Cemetery this autumn morning for Jim Larkin and Maud Gonne and think hard for hunger strikers young and old.

Rooted to the path, a tour guide removes silver spectacles and with a cloth handkerchief wipes them clear of rain. He'd smiled when I sought directions to Brendan Behan's final resting place. An empty pint glass marked the author's headstone's eye.

2.

My aunts gathered at the table had invited me, decades ago, to join them for their game of twilight poker. History/politics was their given subject, whiskey/vodka their drinks of choice. We were country people then and remain so still and have never lacked for sophistication or wit.

By then, I had commenced with foam and razor while spouting harsh opinions. My aunt and godmother lit another menthol cigarette. Others, my mother amongst them, gathered cards and refilled glasses.

Out-of-doors, the breaking waves attached a languorous soundtrack to the flashing Co. Wexford night. If I listened hard to what my aunts revealed, I lost my shirt at cards. I quickly learned to listen as I played. I discovered that four of any kind beats a full house, that Collins, all hands down, was superior to my namesake—De Valera.

3.

Earlier, I had wiped mother's dinner table down and crusted, before cutting into quarters, plates of buttered sandwiches. I sat by the kitchen door awaiting the wave of my aunts' arrival. I am a grown-up of our world these days who plays warm hands they dealt decades ago.

4.

On a rowdy double-decker from Glasnevin Cemetery back into town, I sink down into seat metal and blue plastic, three dead aunts screaming uproarious liquid laughter in my ears. The day brightens. I tap my left foot to the Dublin beat. This racket wrought by teenagers on this bus is the driver's problem, not mine.

My mother lives amongst us still, a single light shining from her bedroom window at the bottom of the hill. More than her sisters, she reasoned as she spoke. She did not drink and ranked superior at cards. A freedom to let go was one gift she has passed along to me.

5.

Now, we have arrived at the great centenary. Pearse, Connolly, Plunket, and all of our great heroes, were called to the GPO to liberate us from the horrors of Saxon servitude. I have descended from the upper saloon, dropped off by Cleary's clock.

Though their names are unnoted on pantheon stone—Kathleen, Teresa, Margaret, Nancy—their wisdom floats, generation to generation, topping each glass, savoring each waiting plate.

Picking Strawberries at Roban's of the Moyne

We headed out
alert and spry
in back of Roban's
rocking trap, the sun was rising
in the sky, the old man
teased the donkey's flank
with the boss
of his walking stick.

At the table
by the gate
a wide-hatted
silver lady yawned;
all of us were handed
pails, told not to gache,
get on with it.

Down the drills
on hands and knees
we moved at speed;
filling buckets was
our task, eating
strawberries as we
pleased.

We broke for lunch
and rallied briefly
after tea. Mrs. Roban
made up fair tallies,
each child's pocket
lined with gold,
we washed our hands
at the cowhouse pump.

We left the country
tired and burned,
our bodies ached
our faces shone.
Anyone recall
the long jaunt home?
Don't ask me! I was
out all stone cold
from farmyard fence
to the Island Road,
in back of Roban's
rocking trap.

Country Life

Stella Phelan's palms offered in greeting
at her kitchen door are white with flour.

Seated now, we drink strong tea, eat warm
scones she has placed on a blue plate

next to the buns we'd found withering
in Mulligan's bakery on the Avenue

in Gorey. We offer each other wry nuggets
of conversation, terms smugly drawn from

bags of clichés as wise as the chipped mugs
we wrap our fingers round. We moan together

when we hear that the Wilsons had called in
last Sunday on the way back from Arklow

shopping, their "fragile" daughter fidgeting
in her purse for sanitizer the minute the table

was set. On wooden forms we sit, old clock
singing out the time. Rain, this day—for it is

summer in Ireland after all—falling on fuchsia
in the garden, we catch this looking up, above

the faces, from time to time, all the better
to wrest perspective. After our cigarettes,

drawn from packets like cold revolvers,
have flared to life deep talk commences.

Our targets today: young people in general,
Republicans, Dubliners' driving habits while

holidaying in the country, and in deference to
Mrs. Lynch, who joins us for the day, anyone

from Co. Carlow. Drinking deeply, we incline
ears: vowel, consonant, rhythm, seanfhocal,

bean an tí, huge bursts of laughter, blue air
Silk Cut regular and ultra, Old Mrs. O'Kelly

held up to ridicule—a woman of her years—
for favouring pints of Smithwicks shandy

over Jameson or G and T. We do not rush
away but linger for encores played out round

the kitchen sink. Stella Phelan ordered now:
"For God's sake woman, please sit down,"

when rising she reaches for a dry tea towel.
Her legs unbuckle, she sinks slowly into rest.

A Fast Five Years Have Passed

A woman sweeps a tiled passageway
of red maple leaves. At her back
fields climb in line to the lunar wave.

Father, I can no longer hear
the stilly night
you oft rehearsed
along Blackstairs' paths
as I tie blue iris to eaves
of this ryokan.

Father, Mt. Leinster's conifers once swung
to the weaves of your melodies

The Nine Stones were warmed
by your werthered breath. Tired
you wrestled me tight to your iron spine.

Father, well-deep your absence
prospers here, bright

with breeze, birdsong, fox, vermillion.

Lightly now, your fingers tug at my cotton sleeve.

Canción: Father's First Day in America

On my father's first day in America
a young couple mounted a super-sized
Sony boombox atop a garbage can
at a bus stop: Dyckman St. & Broadway.
For his enjoyment, they played loud
merengue and danced blithe steps
along the sidewalk they had shaped
to the Dominican beat, and except
for an old dude in a grey mackintosh,
we cheered at entertainment's end,
the bus halting with a cinch and roar.

Next day on a downtown A between
125th and Columbus Circle, a wildly-
dressed young lady called for attention:
she sang a *canción* regarding love,
trabajo, and old sad waves that shatter
as they drop on distant shores, lyrics
forcing up from my father's tender core
a sigh, a tear, a reckoning of many lost
lives, as he saw it, passed in harsh light,
far from hearth and home, his own uncle
disbanded patriot from our troubled times
found dead on an LA skid-row alleyway.

Grinning ear-to-ear, mother sat between us
on the bounding subway car. On the third day
we lunched to the rum-thum-thum of drums
while seated in the shade in Central Park.
We waited among the tourist horde for a wild
corps of Korean break-dancers to resume.

From Here I Whisper Anseo

His hold lessening on earth, father revolved
best amongst women, his forms adhering
to their voices, their elegance while
walking through opened doors whispering
to him of paradise.

                                        August, continent away,
seated on sand and stone, I look east-
ward to imagine him, my dear old man,
sun-burned, his towel, togs, ear-plugs,
glasses, arms reached out better to absorb
late ounces of the sun, all that was offered,
shoulders to water, eyes open to land and sky.

Outside by the open back door seated, our
women absorb length of evening: each holds
a cup and cigarette, the benches painted
white and blue, children lighted out
across lane and meadow, fled like gazelles.

As I await a bus in Albuquerque, mother's
voice pings off purple sage and piñon pine.
Again, it's evening time in Co. Wexford.
Anseo, I whisper, once or twice, onto desert
air. A kite-like word can catch air, ascend
to weigh suspended, bright immigrant star.

Manhattan Wood

Under Manhattan
oaks &

hurled
deciduous rows,

we walk across
Inwood Hill Park

sunlight

shaft falls

old leaves list
on the forest floor

robin on a long ledge
of an upraised limb.

Hello my father
Michael.

Shopakkopoch
language of place
lore of place
salvation
Nine Stones
Bluebell Wood
we walked
one April day

you say, the trees—
you emphasize—are

an alphabet laced
across our land.

At the Gotham Book Mart

i.m. Andreas Brown

Once a young and hopeful scholar
I rushed the Gotham Book Mart's
shelves to seek sundry texts assigned
for seminars; more, in truth, for
old world ambience than supply
of books wrung out. Sometimes,
your eyebrows climbed, Andreas,
on bearing witness to an author's
name in bold print upon my CUNY
syllabus. Once, I asked of you,
"Does Salinger still come in to browse
on odd sorties home to New York?"
"Oh yes," you said. "Ten minutes
ago whilst you were on your knees
amongst the Ms seeking Malamud's
Magic Barrel, Salinger stepped aside
to lend you cleaner access
to the lower shelves." Stern and spry
you then retreated to your annex
at the rear. Sotto voce on your phone.
Gotham Book Mart where I liked to fish.

Sight

I leaned forward, squeezed my eyes
to squint but could not read the lower
lines of letters on the crooked alphabet
pinned to the school's stark wall. Two
adults who observed wore white coats.
I had been called from class,
brought into the infirmary, first to sit
and wait. I was certain I had polio:
this was something worse. I was stupid:
I could not see. Fearing the master's
strap, I leaned forward to weep
onto my knees. I am as thick as a ditch,
at year's end they keep all dunces back.

The lady's hand touched my shoulder
blade, the optometrist appraised me
with a smile. She wiped my face with
a handkerchief. Then, we played a game
of glasses. Which is clearer: A or B?
he asked of me. Not sure? Once more?
A or B, which of these is clearer? A,
I say. I sit straight and confident. Look
at me. World, beware. I can read like you.
I call from top to bottom all letters,
left to right, right to left, up and down
letters that form their funny alphabet.
He gestures. She lifts her hand, stands
back, smiles as she appraises me. A boy
better than the rest, most likely to succeed.

Calligraphy Class

Hunched so tight I shudder
as sparrows cluster
near my backdoor feeder.

Brush dipped, brush raised,
then proper posture shaped,

First thought best thought,
spring as a woodpecker springs.

But, Sensei, how my innards churn.
I'm fixed on error and rebuke,
on sheets that cannot be corrected
or unmade, honed again to primary school.

The Temple of the Golden Pavilion by Yukio Mishima

In Mishima's novel two couples alight in Arashiyama
forecasted to be wet this day in May:
youthful, irritated, in disbelief both men
cocksure their dates cannot flatter as Lady Kogo
had when maple trees were trolling fully into leaf.
The women heave their picnic basket to the river.

The couples wander to the Togetsu Bridge; Kogo's
grave discovered as they loiter by the river.
Today, tourists favor, both women and men,
the slender curvy bamboo walk of Arashiyama:
Look, a late-blooming cherry blossom found in May,
Yukio Mishima's narrator noted turning a new leaf.

'Loving Thoughts of a Husband' was the tune Lady Kogo
played on her harp in sleepy Arashiyama
one autumn night; these old events recalled in May,
spring adding heft and clear décor to path and leaf.
Lady Kugo was true to her regal lover, of other men
she gave no thought, her grave visible by the Hozu River.

West of the Togetsu Bridge it's named the Hozu River
east it must be called Katsura, with rules men
complicate waters shared in Arashiyama.
Yukio Mishima's two young men recite for Lady Kogo
pious sutras warped by whining cries, one maple leaf
incised by such parodies early in the month of May.

Poetry and art are the direst harbingers agree the men,
words that grate like teeth grinding in Arashiyama.
Azaleas are blossoming into purple sleeved rich leaf
as many day-trippers wander distant from the river,
the positive and gay turn to each other as Lady Kogo
had turned to kiss her noble lover many years ago one May.

Osaka Oleander

Petals of red oleander are pinned to stems
as airfoil blades are to propellers shaped.

White oleander opens as a handshake should
on a red leaf path leading inland from Osaka.

Oleander is the flower of Hiroshima, *kyochikuto*
first to rise in bloom after the city had been blitzed

by Enola Gay, Mr. Harkness answers. The citizens

heard across stony hillsides hopeful oleanders'
hue and cry doubling under cloud. They supposed

that Truman's poison would not settle fully down
to sleep. Soon, Japan revived to unsettle the USA.

It is late on an August day. The building's doors
are closing soon. We put our history books away.

In an orange dress, mother waits in the vestibule.
She likes to labor in the garden among her flowers.

Graig Sack Co.

Brick, mortar, frame and floorboard haze.
Burst sunlight folk songs as the Clancys
& Tommy Makem roar from sack store
wireless: workers rounding out racy tunes
with homespun lyrics germane to females
of the town. Burlap by thousands lined
and mounded along driest dun wooden
floors, guarded by Rover, an old Red Setter
for whom haste is a complex term. Cold
granite of St. Aidan's casts shadows
over work and play. Every act sanctified.

In the yard's sunlit space men break to savor
sandwiches served with mustard hot
as a woman's breath inhaled outside
the Scarawalsh marquee. Like my
grandfather, men pull on pipes whilst
hocking hard, spitting still polite so long
as the actor is male and advanced in years.

For barley & salmon, there is but one short
season. Each weaves to rhythms I did not hear
held snugly then in youth's eternity. Years
float on summer's breezes sweet and low.
The Slaney drums homeward spinning flow,
salmon floating secrets we have yet to grow.

Graig's men caress burlap sacks as gently
as they will dry their daughters' faces
with soft towels, Saturday evening darkening
into night, cleaned clothes laid out and ironed
for the cathedral's early Mass. I lie stock-still
amongst a wave of tired boys: flat on sacks,
counting joists, until stirred and shaken,
Graig's Sack Co. becomes Dunnes Stores.

The Malt Stores

A steel-framed colossus rose above the downed malt store:
Pigeons shifted higher to gain

Better spots amid the wreckage, no cats escaping
Bags of poison laid mine-like

Throughout the site. First choked, then shriveled, all
Flowers disappeared to dust.

Completed, open for business, neither grace nor ornament
Much in evidence here

Two boys are spitting gaily at a passing car. The cage
Is steel rivet-shelled

While concrete floors, walls, partitions, light fixtures,
And breezy swinging doors

Fill-out its sturdy frame: Dunnes Stores Better Value
Beats them all in our famed town.

Now, to this mecca beneath the grey cathedral punters
Flock for clothes, food, mops,

Pots and pans and every kind of drink one might dare
To call. As a child, I named

The narrow entrance to Graig Sack Co. the opening
To the underworld, with nail and knife

Tunneling daily many levels down to where I observed,
when she had left us for the dead,

My own grandmother by Charon poled Lethe-ward to her
Rest. Malt and Sack Stores sat side-by-side

On Barrack St. as spokes of the town's ancient inner
Core. A gang of us stretched

On burlaps counting joists and timbers overhead
As below us workers belted out

Latest hits at the height of the 60s ballad boom;
Repertoires repatriated whole

From New York by Clancy Bros. and Tommy Makem.
When the sack store was lost

To progress, the workers scattered with their tunes
Like crows across a neat-knocked

Field, the building quickly razed and counted-out
As a referee would a washed-out

Boxer who had flattered only to deceive. Except at
Harvest time when trailer

Loads of barley were hefted into town, our ancient
And historic core spun into

A quiet decline though I could always detect
In darkest corners odors

Of burlap sack and waft of dryness held in air.
Malters and Graig by this date

By one single outfit owned. Next, to modernize
The malting process

The owners bought a great machine—humming
Night and day—

To occupy the old sack store though not before
Allied and Nazi troops

Had engaged in conflict there: *Underground*
Sabotage! Ambush! Kidnap!

A feature movie, to great delight, being filmed
In our small town.

One night I woke in terror to bang and holy smoke,
The new machine designed

To reduce our street's quiet to smithereens. Owners
Of this great monstrosity,

It is noted in the town's museum, had by marriage
Established some connections

To the Boston Kennedys. Barley being malted: what
Soured the air later

Returning labeled as Power's Gold. First, wedged
Between malting mill

And front room where Marty Wilson cobbled
As he sang, there had been

An old sack store: lately a wrack machine; today,
Dunnes Stores Better Value

Beats them all. Around Marty the little people danced
At the top of Irish St.

Memory leaps to regale me this July afternoon:
Standing beneath the great green sign,

An émigré returned home, to admit that I have lived,
        By absence it is true,

Through many iterations of our town and have bought,
        To be honest, my share of goods

And fill of foods, mass-produced, factory-farmed,
        In big box stores.

I enter with the horde to seek on ordered shelves
        Tins of tuna, loaves of bread,

Some cans of ale to wash all vittles down, fit my soul
        To sell while mourning

The vanished small retailer, who, as sunshine lit an area
        Round his open door,

Stood arrayed—necktie and neat-brushed hair—
        Who was, or had been called,

The future of our nation. As a child I'd watched
        In awe as the Monk Doran's

Staff bore shutters and steel rods to elegantly seal
        From view the innards

Of their rich emporium. Today, many shops
        Along our ancient streets—

Weafer, Rafter, named for patriots—lie derelict
        And dark. I remember Simon Kehoe,

My friend's father, stepping from shop to curb
        To discuss sports, eager to hear

News brought fresh to town by those who had
Lately idled in

From the countryside; Nora Cleary in her tavern
Across the street mixed

That savage elixir—Smithwicks and red lemonade—
No talk of age restriction,

The landlady like many of that era strictly libertarian.
Jack Dunne once allowing me

Bring home from Bourke-Roche's a pair of trousers
On approval. As children,

We bore silent witness in Daniel Bolger's Dept. Store
As documents and notes

Were raced pneumatically through golden pipes,
The staff obliging of our presence,

Quietly we sat, all the better to observe. On Slaney St.
Parking was freely legal

On both sides. I do not make the case that our world
Was so much better then:

I breathed misery fragrant in the air and quickly
For myself sought out

More benign foreign shores. Mass production brings,
Though its price is hidden,

Some part of what we like to label democracy.
I see but few of the grizzled

And hateful faces today that often blocked my path
When I, no doubt, one child

Too easily rattled, sought to cross The Market Square.
Bankers, lending only to mighty stores,

Have stripped away at our gorgeous and most historic
Town. Throughout I sense an air

Of gloom tightening to deep despair as young adults
Commence the short first leg

To OZ by boarding the Wexford Bus, one last look
Shot across the quay

At Norman castle and Cotton Tree Café, where kin
To me, push bravely

Against the bitter waters of *The Great Recession.*
Twelve years long since

Joyful the new millennium rang, a sour troika haunt
Our noble town. How

Rich republics when women never get to bounce
Grand babies on their knees.

In a rush, I gather my purchases from Dunnes Stores:
Green signs floating shore to shore.

July 12th, Gorey, Co. Wexford

Our town went orange for a day.
Two lads reached into Daly's garden
to feast on his nasturtiums. Sexton
Smyth, ski-hat concealing close-shaved
crown, peered down New Line Rd.
at a line of streetlights, yellow
with a hint of orange. Nora Phelan
left her mother's home wrapped
head-to-toe against wind and rain,
her orange purse inside an Aldi
shopping bag. All enraged, old
Robbie Dowd beat an orange flag
outside Sinn Féin HQ. In Gwalia
Stores, Rosie Dolan's Coke
metamorphosed into Fanta Orange.
Global warming the culprit here
insisted Ken Berry to Biddy Crowe.
They saw Nora Phelan of Parnell
Drive fly gobsmacked through her
orange hall. Look, Rev. Sally Graham,
all dolled-up, crossing Patriot Sq.:
orange Hermes scarf though that
turquoise dress her coupe-de-grace.

A Mariner Returns to Inwood

The elder's short chin it was
that drew us in. He'd walked
across the street and harked
at us in greeting. His wrinkled
face was warped like weathered
timber ripped from a home's
westward leaning gable. Aged
to outline, seated now amongst
us on our brownish city bench,
we older urbanite idle men like
faint daggers on display. He said
"For thirty years I have lived
among foreigners, drank rum
in portside bolt holes, Santiago
to Cape Verde. Listen up. I seek
an audience for my tales."

An
omnibus had halted at the lights
by a garbage can, two pigeons
wrestled with a candy wrapper.
"I am a native of this place,"
intoned our ghostly interloper.
"The voices have all changed,"
he declaimed, "my old bodega,
lo and behold, flipped to House
of Sushi." A sailor this man
had been, for many decades
flung about from the Maritimes
to Asia's Philippines, Hector
Alvarez, first baseman long ago
for Lincoln H.S.'s winningest
teams. Switching into Spanish,
we joked of a great America
Donald J. Trump did not know

and whistled sweet trans-
gressive airs hot off the melting
pot. Even dust blown upward
from the trampled path we
thankfully inhaled, Hector's
words we brandished like a hot
and newly polished sword.

Awake

At river bend a channel twist,
        tyres on blacktop, moniker
at railway line: nightingale.

I awake under cypresses
        sun passes over roof shingles
Riverbend sub-division: Hearth.

We have winter light to feast on
        hearts modestly concealed
great gales bend limbs, our dreams.

Freights idle at the switching yard
        as I spin slowly world-ward;
sharp, pliantly humble, mocking bird.

Across the hall, my son's old cat
        sleeps on. He is my life.
Ancestors, help wind our story onward.

The Salary Man Comes Home

Don't forget the moon, my love,
please let it never wax nor wane
concealed all day hand-in-glove
it guards forever our darkening plain.

Don't forget our child, my love,
inside or suited for out-of-doors
she likes to tug at your woolen sleeve
releasing to air your secret spores.

Don't forget the bread, my love,
mother bakes it rich and brown
her skirts are gathered at her knees
her wheaten meal is of great renown.

Oh, my love, the road is long
these bureaucrats my days prolong.
Don't neglect to hoard me treats
Look: winter's finally in retreat.

Oh, my love, money's not short
our way winds through forests dark
willows lean low, lovely and smart
we won't carve letters on cypress bark.

Now, the captain's turned on full lights
he's finally found the turn for home
Oh, my love, it's my great delight
to view our cathedral's golden dome.

Writing on the Wall

I will not depart the cinema
until the last dark credits bleed.

My heart holds fast to screen,
to your Dr. Pepper, my Diet Coke,
to an oval of gum affixed under
armrest of Row D, seat 5. Pinkish.
It is late afternoon I think. Correct,
the matinee has just concluded.

But just because I can't depart
the cinema as soon as credits
begin to roll should not indicate
superiority. I am no film buff
nor Pauline Kael look-a-like
who gathers cinematographers'
names to drop onto the coffee
break like learned ogham stones.

Rather, like a kiss received, I
like to linger here while I absorb
lip-balm softly morph to memory.

Finally, a broom-boy beating debris
into dustpan heralds permission
to gather up and go. Do you still
recall how that great percussive boom
held us tight a moment after the Rank
Org's. gong had reached all corners
of our childhood's Astor auditorium?

William Faulkner's Rowan Oak

It is late morning in Oxford
cedar and oak as August casts a fiery glaze
across the spooned-out parking lot.

Here,
we absorb fragrances inhaled and sold:
I grew-up drab decades following
our own Civil War.

Parched familiarities
suffocate and spin as late morning we stroll
arm-in-arm the Rowan Oak of Wm. Faulkner.

Long bereft
of ladies' airs, today's Rowan Oak's
a dusty death trap frying pan.

Colonel Robert Sheegog
a Scotch-Irish planter from Tennessee,
an immigrant like me, raised this home
from Princess Hoka's Chickasaw trail of tears.

A tourist
visiting from Missouri, I inscribe my mark
in the visitors' book though my heart leans
toward the interstate ahead, and lunch.

Marks on the Doorframe

A blind-pulled twilight he marks
his child's height to the doorframe
of her room, registering in her name
dinnseanchas, her shrieks bringing
fall evening light alive, light of evening
as we knew, skin from bath translucent,
as her room catches rhythm of silver
maples rocking back and forth
on westerlies slow along California St.,
her mother firming her one daughter
with the promise of grilled cheese
and hot chocolate cup. On the earth
our wood-framed house is grounded.
We have come to Nebraska to grow.

With care, he makes measurements,
his child being kin to rivers, breath,
measure of this moment penciled
straight. For one evening—if spared
dear Lord—we are a river holding
still. Our lives have not been wasted,
our tastes are sweet as Amish peaches
picked from straw baskets on summer days.

Just To Say, Mr. President

i.m. Pete Hamill

At work in the 1980s under Reagan just as
the laws began to change, my boss at John
Jay College, where I adjuncted for a wage,
aired a long preamble of apology before
seeking for review my squat blue Green Card.

Today, I hear it reported on the morning news
that America is full, that soon the dancing feet
of Inwood Hill and Central Park will be squeezed
like Grey Poupon through narrow gaps carved
into our President's magnificent border wall.

We bring sad songs and ancient eclogues, a rustling
elegance of dress, a learned eloquence of speech.

That Man in Viareggio Is You

Who's that man, twenty-six
in '81 who carries asphodels
through sun-split alleys, marking
tender geographies of Viareggio?
He's singing as he walks, walking
as he sings out autumn syllables
drilled to memory from class
in Viareggio, tart lyrics of an old
canzone of flowers withering
in a vase of woes? Does his heart
burst into rapture as he strides
as cavalier and warbler, drawn to
center earth? Who's that man
that shade conceals, daylight
dropping like a marble to water,
who can find neither verb, noun,
nor adverb, who last week lifted
a woman's hand from her counter,
turning it carefully to examine
a palm lined as a page torn
from a Tuscan scroll? Did Natalia
offer a sly grin before printing
as a gift the digits of her father's
phone to the receipt's reverse?
Was it here in Viareggio, 1981,
amid the quiet push and murmur
that he sought voice? Did he make
a journey here by boat and train
as he'd said to her before turning
to depart the bakery on Via XX
Settembre, *Ti chiamo pomeriggio*,
hoping the casual stress defied
hot flavors pounding head to toe?
Are you that man, twenty-six
in '81, or do you draw from a well
the opening credits of another's life?

Hawk

One long and pencil slender limb
shoots right-angled out
from a peeling sycamore
seven metres overhead. At its pointed finger's
end is perched one stone silent
drop dead gorgeous white-tailed hawk.

There is no movement to discern
save for a soft blush of feather
fluffed by this December wind.

This stretch opens my daily walking route.

Do you see me? Of course
you do though you do not mark me
as wader, locust, mouse, or lusty cardinal.

I am a rambler of no importance.

Shoulder to wheel, eyes on brown ties,
you scour the railroad for a tasty meal.
My gawking does not define you.
I dare not ask for a whisper of your name.

I Hear Everything

I hear rain dropping from a sycamore on Glen Rd;
I hear an owl in an evergreen hoot in the voice of my grandfather;
I hear that the box turtle calls out for me down by the railroad tracks;
Deuce, I hear a player shout from the tennis court;
I hear birdsong everywhere I go;
I hear the man before I see him coming, his portable tuned to Limbaugh;
I hear the boys' and girls' shouts from their hideout in the corner of their yard;
I hear a cat insisting that the front door be opened, yesterday;
I hear the Missouri River Runner's whistle and it is hardly lonesome;
I hear that someone's going somewhere between Kirkwood and KC: it ain't me;
I hear that the wineries in Hermann are open again for business;
I hear pin oaks and maples having a conversation, I eavesdrop;
I hear that there are folks who understand tree language, I am learning;
I hear the consent of tomatoes as they are picked and placed in a basket;
I hear water exiting an aluminum pipe, entering Deer Creek;
Drink this liquid and you will die, I hear the mayor of Maplewood say;
I hear the boys shout at their fishing lines;
I hear the crack of ball on bat, father and son, St. Louis a baseball town;
I hear the rush of traffic on Laclede;
I hear that I don't have to care about all that nonsense on TV.
Stay home, write a poem, is what I hear;
I hear agitated cardinals cry out under the wings of a hawk;
I hear the question you ask when I get home;
You are slow to answer is what I'll hear. Heard nothing. Saw nothing. Schoolboy.

The Pandemic Blows Across Webster Groves

The pandemic we grow used to blows skyward
from rooftops on Pacific
to the pin oaks and maples fixed
harder to the border, wrought
between asphalt and railroad.
It never settles longer than a starling resting.

The backyards are roaring with children.

It's Wednesday? It's not Wednesday? Which day,
you say? Again, the humidity climbs as high
as it had risen yesterday by noon. Or does it just
hold constant like a day lit
by ennui, a fact slipping into caveat?

The spell has been blown across Pacific.
The king's hue is orange and blue,
his face a guttural mess. A crew comes
to harden the border between asphalt and railroad.

They sit on their porches on Pacific.
The mailman is late, the freight's broken down.
No visitors. No meetings for coffee. It is too late
for prayer and too early for vodka and tonic.

It Is Solved by Walking in St. Louis

Today I ramble Deer Creek Greenway,
I skirt Barnickel's tennis courts, I crunch
along the path rehearsing songs, I drive
my girlfriend's Pontiac on blue highways
Tucson to Tucumcari, Lowell George,
burnt country rolling by. Believe it or not,
I am the wild suburban troubadour of rock.

Neighbors acknowledge my daily trundle;
they nod and weave as they rumble
their private pathways through the suburb.
We are stick-figures drawn by L.S. Lowry,
birdsong drowning out the daft of Zoom.
I'm just an excitable boy singing on the fly.

I hit my stride downhill, shift a foot
from Starman to Pretty Vacant to writers
stored like acorns —Chatwin, Murphy,
Morris, Theroux—the paths they carved
by bike, train, bus, and boat traversed
my Dublin bedsit, Cohen turning stereo,
long winter nights I trawled across Old
Pat Brady's threadbare red carpet. I turn
a corner, swing left, cross the bridge
into Rocket Ship Park. My repertoire gives
my age away but I will not be counted out:
I am the choicest of singing walking men,
a witness to the Starmen waiting in the sky.

The Music of the Suburb

There is a fine home on a quiet street
nearby, remodeled head to toe, shingle
to downspout down, night-time all aglow.

How many bathrooms, how bright and high
the foyer only my wife or daughter
could know? They sit up late pandemic
nights reprising episodes of the cable
home improvement show. I have no time
for the sorrow of interior decoration.
I have come to live here from another nation.

There is an elegance to suburbia
that only of late I have feigned to appreciate.
In the past when asked it had been to sigh
by dint of apology when I had to admit
to being a long-time resident of Webster Groves.
I have come here from a close-knit town.
We lived together tightly as a pod of peas.
It was our sad remit: we sometimes came to blows.

I am very comfortable taking long flights
on crowded airplanes overseas. The pandemic's
curbed my travel to this daily suburban
crawl. Jittery. By fright paralyzed, I trawl
for anecdotes to draw my spouse's favor
when I get home. Often, I am forced to cross
against the traffic to avoid the hale
who surge into my own taut space like fleas.
Perhaps a tragic incident will unfold though
this is a little much to ask of Webster Groves.

I walk on. I am wary of dogs and a lover of trains.
I reach a fine home on a quiet street
that I will call Victorian, three elegant stories
climb to hang together in the trees. Remodeled
head to toe, shingle to downspout down,

night-time all aglow. Today, chairs are settled
on the lawn. The florist's van's parked
curbside while wait-staff lay tables
beneath a most gay canopy, mid-November

Thanksgiving almost nigh. Where I grew up
the skies were always gray, summer was done
and busted by the longest day. A wedding!

In the absent manner of late afternoon
with time to kill till cocktail hour
my gaze strays to a lower-level room
where I note a Martin mounted,
its soft browns ebbing the severity
of sharp-white paint, the guitar lending
a soft accent to this large reception room,
in the argot of the home improvement show.

Unlikely that this is home to troubadours
given its aura of affluence
though I am hopeful that musicians
are invited here to perform. I walk home
joyful, my heart rambling through Granada,
my terrified pandemic soul bathed
in Federico Garcia Lorca's gypsy spells:

Verde que te quiero verde.
Verde viento. Verdes ramas.
El barco sobre la mar
y el caballo en la montaña.

A home with a guitar is for sure a fine
suburban home. In the mood, my wife
strums a fine guitar, chords played just as they
should be played on her own Martin guitar.
In Webster Groves the suburb we all call home.

Trampoline

Where she'd once leaped, spun, looped
and flopped, hair and arms
akimbo, Tinsley now sits slow
as a Buddha or mendicant, her eyes
strained to pandemic laptop at school
on her giant trampoline, shade cast
by pin oaks and hardy maples,
air cut by the first fall breezes
blown eastward from Kansas and Colorado.

Tinsley at work brings calm and balm
to my pandemic heart. Ms. Hays
calls out from locked-down Avery Elem.
her hands guide lessons, float PowerPoints
from schoolhouse to Tinsley's trampoline.

It's her mind's motion, her heart's attention,
the wind's cool aspiration that rocks,
though gently, this pre-teen's trampoline.

It's September so Missouri's dry
and warm. Tinsley's learning though
she's escaped from school. She's
seated on a trampoline, she's placed
her laptop on her knees, her red hair
moving on the breeze. Remember,
sad compatriots, school's first day:
somnambulating Millpark Rd
metre by sour metre as heat was sucked
from morning, hope evaporated
from tender hearts. Is it Mathematics
my neighbor ponders or some topic
that hits my liking button more:
The Battle of Gettysburg or Custer
beaten at The Little Big Horn?
Two metres is the mantra for this pandemic
but three cheers for Tinsley absorbing all
seated on her trampoline.

Roscoe Mini-Aussie I.M.

I walk through the Show-Me-State
with Roscoe to whom the oleander
is lethal. Where the park's perimeter greets
the Osage Trail, he pauses a moment
moving homeward. These Missouri oleanders
that climb a wooden fence nearby
are *nerium oleander, laurel de jardin,*
rosa Francesca, jia zhu tao, dogbane, in Irish
oiliander, hailed by cranks to offer a cure
for cancer. Roscoe pauses another moment
to account for me, to register how
to one another we are linked, dog and man,
to affirm my spoke on his turning wheel,
the manner of my gait, what measure
he can gauge of my Monday composition,
the scratched crockeries of my walking day.
I am not half as smart as I pretend to be.

Postcards from Missouri

October 2020

Does the pandemic
deepen
your soul's tenor
or does it drive you
to despise
your neighbor's leaf
blower, and dry
demeanor
a soupçon more?

*

December 2019

My wife crossed the mezzanine
in the Melbourne airport
to visit a pharmacy.

She purchased a package of masks.

I sat on a soft seat in the terminal
reading a novel

while Australia burned.

*

July 4th, 2020, Barnickel Park:

I stand still with you,
box turtle.

Soon a crew
will gather:
let's shuttle together

find a soft spot,
wait
their celebrations out.

*

Meramec River, April 2020

I cast

for a softer breath

when the moon rises

                    I stall

*

New Year's Eve, 2020
28°F

Drafts flush
through the old house's
stripped-out seals

City streets
are prepped for snow

Few follow the road.

Dear Friends,
wherever you rest
this night,

I am quite content.

Red-Winged Blackbirds

Through field glasses
I observe one small flock
of red-winged blackbirds
busy about the Audubon
Center,

          the viewer narrowing
space to single frame
while dreadlock lines crossing
over top whir rhythm sweet
as monks might chant compline.

Seed has been rattled to earth,
grasses through lens magnified.

Of wind, grass and bird sound
no hard register rebounds indoors
though as song I intuit warbling
ear to ear, sweet as a lover's purr.

Nowhere: guns, booty, murder,
mayhem, not even the whizz-
cut of an automobile.

                    Like my
grandmother, the red-winged
blackbirds do no harm. We sit
in the 1960s side-by-side
at the kitchen table drinking tea
afternoon running along
as its own great fearless river.

                    At my back
today, two miles away, swoons
tide together confluence

of the Missouri and Mississippi
Rivers—red-winged blackbirds
returning to the frame to feed.

Grandmother taught me to be
for silence watchful and how
to merge with it, then float away.

I Wheel Your Bedside Table into Place

When the day's last eye is dotted
and the kettle's filled for morning

I wheel your bedside table into place,

recall a neighbor's work on Macy's
Christmas windows in Herald Sq.

He was an adept arranger of nutcrackers
and elves; everything shaped into place.

I plan this night's arrangement

as over platters of meats
your hands once guided into place
slices of ham curled delicately
as bows shaped into communion hair.

There are gifts that cannot be taught
tremors of craft grafted in place.

I take a breath.

Half-full glass of orange juice
flip-phone
tissues
brace of hearing aides
full glass of water
rosary beads.

Your night's companions
are as delicately placed as the many feasts
you shaped for dignitary and bride
at Murphy-Floods Hotel,

I flatter myself to think.

There is little left to say
except to repeat again
the little words that line our hearts.

I raise the bed rail. Secure you.
I turn the oxygen system on.
Hear its reassuring hum.

What a blessing it has been
to have passed another day with you
to have retrieved my place
beside you, walking Uptown to 42nd Street.

The Old Hotel in the Market Square

1.

Rubble and dust have settled down, a clock
circles firm monotony above the town.
Local people walk street-side of the striped
hoarding to which bill-posted invitations cling.
Discharged now in walkers' eyes, the dust
bedded down by rain: all accept this hotel site
is derelict. Next weekend, posted bills declare,
buses leave for Knock at half-past nine.
An English circus will soon arrive in town.
Church bells call all uphill one more time:
Enniscorthy's faithful hailed to Lenten prayer.

2.

In the capital city of diesel and feta cheese,
on a high stool over a drafting board,
an architect knows that to draw is to make
flesh. He left his village to seek in the capital
the certain curve of steel, the marble cool,
the view from the café window of the south-
bound traffic. He reveres all that promises
inaction, evasion, erasure. Rural towns
are the *terra nullius* on which he invents
the future. He sees rain falling on capped
heads in washed-out corners of the state.

3.

In these washed-out corners of the nation,
no child knocks on the old storyteller's door,
the piano teacher has turned her face
to the garden wall to count the climbing slugs,
no one volunteers to write our history down.
The chorus has departed another rural town.

4.

The bank manager's great oak desk
is fixed to block the narrative of the town.
He has placed on his full-deep trousers
many charts and maps and a horny
sheaf of multi-coloured envelopes:
his lap remains a zone of coolest cool.
He taps his keyboard as old prints
of planter houses that formed a backbone
of the town gather dust about his yellow
walls. There's a twiddling of thumbs,
a sigh, a call to coffee with the staff,
a pause on a downward step to ponder
a five-iron struck at dog-leg number nine
when he flirted, for one shining moment,
with the captain's prize. His assistant
lets the manager know that a developers'
queue has formed in the lane outside—
Dublin designates retail the hotel site.
Quakers, who were they? He will seek
an explanation, their initials posted high
on fieldstone throughout the Market Sq.

5.

From my far-suburban home, on the distant
fringes of our capital, I am making a brief
return to Enniscorthy to conduct a day
of business with a well-known merchant
of the town. On a bench in Market Square,
with an hour to kill, I share an Abrakebabra
take-a-way with an old man, ragged
and wise: he is seated tight beside me on a rise.

6.

In truth, the old man says, all towns remain
contested ground, and all of us have of late
been compromised though it would seem
churlish to complain: every year I see my
pension rise and, for no good reason, it is
raised many hundred euro more. He wears
a Garda surplus overcoat, Jack Charlton hat,
pulls hard on an old clay pipe. Be careful
not to judge too harshly, he scolds me, when
I wave my hand toward the derelict site
before indicating, right next to it, a gaudy
sign lit-up to raise awareness of American cuisine.

7.

The old hotel is much alive in me, the old man says,
the burgers at Thunder Road Café are best
when moistened with a squeeze of burger sauce.
Though that vacant site across the way
might seem to you a no-man's-land, our town
cannot be reckoned a Van Diemen's Land: you
should not count locals here as Aboriginals.
I climbed three steps to the foyer on my wedding
day: for many years, I returned to the hotel's
lounge there to play; my fiddle tuned, my bow ready
to strike for all the rebel note. Our old town
you forsook, my brave bucko, now here you are returned
to lecture and harshly criticize—he flourished as he rose.
He flung our kebab wrappers toward the middle
of the Market Square. Long-versed in city ways,
I sought out the always most elusive rural rubbish bin.

Don’t Go Back to Courtown Harbor

Coke-bellied boats are afloat
under a fair-haired autumn sky,

two boys lounge back, arched
toward warp-stone harbor wall,
sea-washed scattered brown.

Hue of goats to westward hill
latched—like doors in motion.

Washing lines whipped by gusts
that rush-in off the Irish Sea.

                                        I distill today
the Bayview’s scuttled hulk,
the undone path to Joe’s Café
where we sat under framed
Elvis drinking Fanta fizz.

                                                    I read
your face signs, softly touched
your right-hand’s chill thin fingers,
fresh and open as a dreaming child’s.

These decades pass, layer, petrify:
warm days are memories of hats;
Sally’s was white, my father’s
mariner blue. Her image
like a breath of smoke pushed
early into eternity, my father’s plume
evaporating quietly one Sunday
morning in Wexford Hospital
from nine decades of play. We are
kings or queens or courtiers for a single day.

The World Is Busy While We Are Having Lunch

I begin the luncheon preparations late.
I wash and rinse the vegetables,
place a slice of ham across each plate.

You watch me cut cucumber and tomato,
gouge seeds from a yellow pepper, hunched
over the bin. I pass you lettuce and cold potatoes

and lodge a cutting board and sharp knife
on the table center right. Moving your hands
you settle each as you might right a startled child.

I am not hungry though I'll eat with you today.
Is the kettle boiled? Have you sliced the loaf?
There's coleslaw hiding in the fridge, look

behind the punnet of blueberries on the left.
When the food is chopped and matched, she
turns her palms open like a priest's. Mother,

these are the happiest hours I have passed with you;
we talk round the corners of our lives, doors
closed against the gale, hearts disarmed and hale.

The world is at work. Other sons rush Tesco
to snag a pizza slice and a swig of Coke. The ropy
winter's light is fading. We eat, we drink, we talk.

Dream, Wife, Lake Superior

We sleep under old timbers
that creak from the buoyancy of salt
groan from oaths of dead kin

we drift on bucked by Somnus
as low hours burn and hurl
at the margins of sight
as night drops by hours into glass.

The News Tribune is yellowed
and stained, sand shifts
to daybreak. Longshoremen stand ready
to haul us to our posts on the quay

as waking and dreaming, of water
and sea, of rage and retreat, of many
and few, of men on a pier who turn
from our cries called from the bow
of the Edmund Fitzgerald, gales blown

through the hollows of flesh
dropped from each face, flag wet
on the mast, flag on our duvet damp.

Crept close under timbers, our names
water the paper's dark print, night dips
to the east. The sun will rise as before
is a song that I hear on your breath.

I loosen my grip from your frame and exhale.

Rock Island

The road along the river sways to Rock Island.
        Towns passed through along the way
to Rock Island sing in the slower registers that never
        ask to be remembered
though diction sweetened on the breeze and rhymes
        folded find favor with honeysuckle
and fleur-de-lis, and like a woman finger-picking
        an old guitar, waves
pucker along the Mississippi. Traffic crosses
        from Hannibal into Illinois.

We motor north through Canton and Palmyra,
        Ft. Madison, Burlington.
Highway 61 divides at city limits, links up again
        on the northern sides.
The children read names with such precision
        it seems each place name
is now a legend raised on a Roman scroll. Cities
        then drop like moisture
dried from asphalt after furious thunderstorms.

        I pick Americana to play
when their voices fade to the rhythm of the ride.
        Is it right to think
the gifted left Keokuk while shut-in citizens
        settled-in for Friday
fish-fries at St. Joseph's and bowling/bingo
        Saturdays at eight?
In a far field I take heed of beds of grasses
        bowed near the trunk
of a cottonwood; are we too far to the east
        of the Tall Grass Prairie
for a sight of the Little Bluestem of the Loess Hills?

Remember that road trip,
I call out above the music? But my family is asleep.
I am quite alone, no longer
careful. So I cry to the wrenching lyrics, a loved man
among strangers. South
of Muscatine soft lines of light are crossed by the flight
of water. I grew up tight
in a river town where the narrow streets ran serpentine
to the Slaney. Rock Island, 30 miles.

Footbridge to Maplewood

slack water
caught
in shadow warp
of winter trees

iced over

moments
I stand
on the footbridge
to draw breath
with ancestors

I cross

hawks' breasts
white on the limb
impassive, imperial

I walk

swivel
through a stile
as minutes
drop into an hour.

I return

the ice has melted

the sky is open
the sun's warming

everything is turning.

Notes

'Yola Sprong.' and 'Sprong.' Sprong is the term used in Co. Wexford for pitchfork. It is a word carried over from the Yola dialect. People will tell you in Wexford that a sprong and a pitchfork are not one and the same. Yola, as Sascha Santschi-Cooney points out in *The Fort and Bargy Dialect*, "was a dialect of the West Germanic branch of languages (which includes English, German, and Dutch), formerly spoken in the two south-eastern baronies of Wexford called Forth and Bargy." Though Yola had vanished as a vernacular by the late 18th century, it retains an important place in how language is spoken in Co. Wexford. The term sprong is just one example of a part of Yola being carried forward into the present. 'Yola Sprong' is a loose version of my own poem translated into the Yola dialect. I am indebted to Sascha Santschi-Cooney's work.

'The Temple of the Golden Pavilion by Yukio Mishima.' Yukio Mishima's *The Temple of the Golden Pavilion* was first published in Japan in 1956. Arashiyama lies northwest of Kyoto. The tombstone of the Heike courtesan Lady Kogo of Sagano is found here.

'The Malt Store.' For generations, an industrial site in Enniscorthy embracing Barrack St. and parts of Irish St. and Island Rd., that housed a malting enterprise as well as Graig Sack Co., a business that rented out burlap sacks to farmers. The area also embraced family homes and other businesses, including Marty Wilson's shoemaker's shop. The site was redeveloped and repurposed as a Dunnes Store in 2006. Parts of the original structure have been retained. *Underground* (1970), directed by Arthur H. Nadel, was filmed in Enniscorthy. Some scenes were filmed at the Malt Store. The film was set in occupied France during World War Two.

'Manhattan Wood.' Shopakkopoch is a ceremonial rock in Inwood Hill Park at the northern tip of Manhattan. Legend has it that this was the location in 1626 where Peter Minuit, representing the Dutch East India Company, purchased the island from Seyseys, the leader of the Canarsee tribe of Native Americans, for 60 guilders worth of goods ($24).

'William Faulkner's Rowan Oak.' Rowan Oak was William Faulkner's home in Oxford, Mississippi. It is now a museum.

'The Old Hotel in the Market Square.' Originally, Murphy-Flood's Hotel, a business started by Annie Murphy, my grandmother. Currently, after a fire, in ruins. Our family home on Barrack St. was right behind it, connected by a passageway.

Acknowledgements

Some poems included in this collection were originally published in the following newspapers and literary journals. Sincere thanks to the editors and sponsors of these publications.

American Journal of Poetry; Backstory Journal; The Blue Nib; The Café Review; Canadian Journal for Irish Studies; Cold Mountain Review; Connotations Press; Crannóg; Cyphers; Dappled Things; Galway Review; Hubbub; The Irish Times; Naugatuck River Review; Other Terrain Journal; Poetry Ireland Review; Prairie Schooner; Reading Ireland; The Stony Thursday Book; The Waxed Lemon.

Poems also appeared in the following anthologies:

Pat Boran ed. *Local Wonders: Poems of Our Immediate Surrounds.* Dublin: Dedalus Press, 2021.

Nathalie F. Anderson ed. *Open-Eyed, Full-Throated: An Anthology of American-Irish Poets.* Dublin: Arlen House, 2019.

Alan Hayes ed. *Hodges-Figgis Bookshop 250th Anniversary Anthology.* Dublin: Arlen House, 2018.

Maria Nolan ed. *From Wexford with Love: Focal-Wexford Literary Festival.* Focal and Alzheimer Society of Ireland, 2015.

Helena Mulkerns ed. R*ed Lamp, Black Piano.* Dublin: Tara Press, 2013.

Thanks to Geraldine Mills, Paul O' Reilly, Susan Millar DuMars, Greg Delanty, and Drucilla Wall for their detailed feedback and editorial skills. Thanks to Jules McCue for the cover image. Thanks to Jessie Lendennie and Siobhán Hutson Jeanotte for their support over the years.

EAMONN WALL's poetry collections include *Dyckman-200th Street* (1994), *The Crosses* (2000), *Sailing Lake Mareotis* (2011), and *Junction City: New and Selected Poems* (2015), all published by Salmon Poetry. In addition to poetry, Eamonn Wall has contributed essays and reviews to newspapers and journals including the *Chicago Tribune*, the *Washington Post*, the *Irish Times*, *Reading Ireland*, the *Irish Literary Supplement*, *Berfrois* and other publications. His prose books are *From the Sin-e Café to the Black Hills: Notes on the New Irish*, winner of the Durkan Award from the American Conference of Irish Studies; *Writing the Irish West: Ecologies and Traditions*; and *From Oven Lane to Sun Prairie: In Search of Irish America.* He edited two volumes of James Liddy's essays for Arlen House and co-edited *Coleridge and Contemplation* for *Poetica* (Japan). Eamonn Wall is a past-president of the American Conference for Irish Studies and from 2014-19 served as a vice-president of Irish American Writers and Artists Inc., an organization founded to encourage Irish Americans to get involved in the arts. He was chosen as the Heimbold Chair in Irish Studies at Villanova University in 2014. For 2023, he has been selected as a fellow in non-fiction by the Writers' Institute of the City University of New York-Graduate Center. A native of Enniscorthy, Co. Wexford, Eamonn Wall has lived in St. Louis for the past two decades. He works at the University of Missouri-St. Louis, teaching English and directing community outreach to the Irish American community and study abroad for UMSL Global, the university's international studies unit.

Photo: August H. Jennewein

salmonpoetry
Cliffs of Moher, County Clare, Ireland

"Publishing the finest Irish and international literature."
Michael D. Higgins, President of Ireland